Edward Sherman Gould

Practical hydraulic Formulæ

For the Distribution of Water through long Pipes

Edward Sherman Gould

Practical hydraulic Formulæ
For the Distribution of Water through long Pipes

ISBN/EAN: 9783337106393

Printed in Europe, USA, Canada, Australia, Japan

Cover: Foto ©ninafisch / pixelio.de

More available books at **www.hansebooks.com**

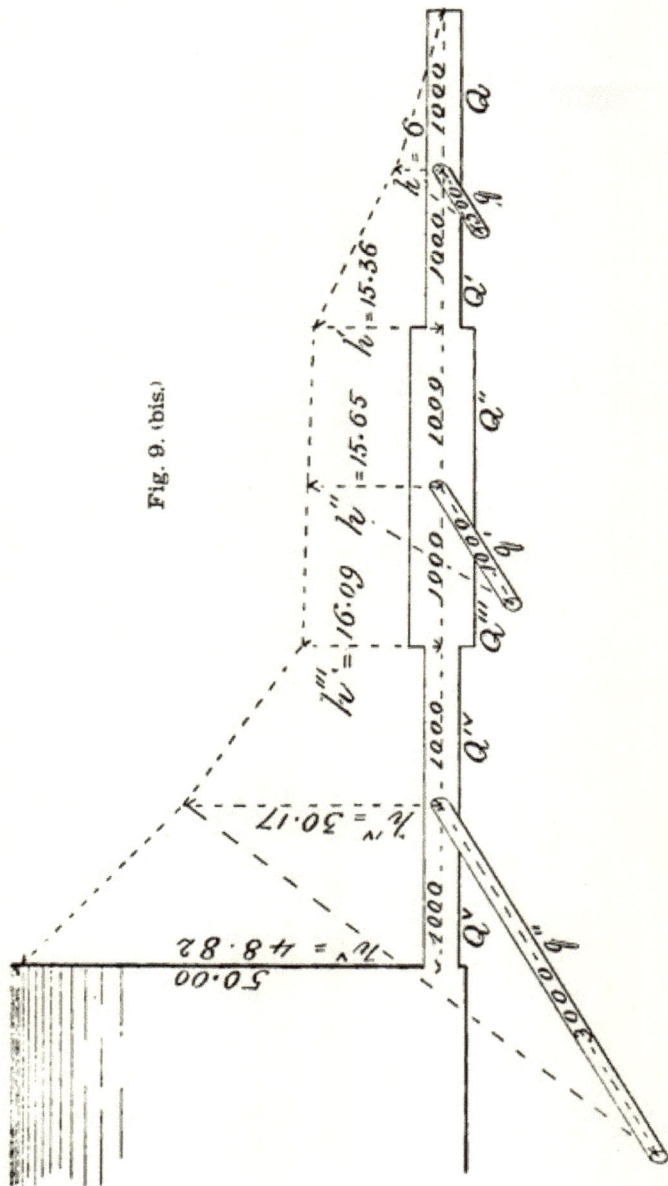

Fig. 9. (bis)

$k' = 9.74$

Q

q

Q'

$h_1 = 15.36$

Q''

$h'' = 15.65$

q'

Q'''

$h''' = 16.09$

Q^{iv}

$h^{iv} = 30.17$

Q^v

q''

$h^v = 48.82$

50.00

1000 1000 1000 1000 1000 1000 1000

3000

PRACTICAL

HYDRAULIC FORMULÆ

FOR THE

Distribution of Water Through Long Pipes.

BY

E. SHERMAN GOULD,

M. AM. SOC. C. E.

Consulting Engineer to the Scranton Gas and Water Co.

NEW YORK:

ENGINEERING NEWS PUBLISHING CO.

1889.

INTRODUCTION.

The following pages first appeared as a series of articles in the columns of ENGINEERING NEWS. They are now republished with a few corrections and additions.

In virtue of the law of gravitation, water tends naturally to pass from a higher to a lower level, and without a difference of level there can be no natural flow.

It can be said in all seriousness—although the statement may seem to invite the unjust accusation of an ill-timed attempt at pleasantry—that the whole science of hydraulics is founded upon the three following homely and unassailable axioms:

First. That water always seeks its own lowest level.

Second. That, therefore, it always tends to run down hill, and

Third, that other things being equal, the steeper the hill, the faster it runs.

In the case of water flowing through long pipes, the hill down which it tends to run is the HYDRAULIC GRADE LINE. If the pipe be of uniform diameter and character, the hydraulic grade line is a straight line joining the water surfaces at its two extremities, provided that the pipe lies wholly below such straight line, and its declivity is measured—like that of all hills--by the ratio of its height to its length.

But if there be any changes whatever in the pipe, either of diameter or in the nature of its inside surface; or if there be increase or diminution of the volume of water entering it at its upper extremity by reason of branches leading to or from the main pipe, then the hydraulic grade line becomes broken and distorted to a greater or less extent, so that its declivity is not uniform from end to end, but consists of a series of varying grades some steeper than others though all sloping in the same direction.

As regards the third axiom, the proviso—" other things being equal "—must not be overlooked. For we shall find that a pipe of greater diameter but less hydraulic declivity than another, may give a greater velocity to the water passing through it. Also, of two pipes of the same hydraulic slope and diameter, the one having the smoother inside surface affords the greater velocity.

The vertical distance from any point in a pipe to the hydraulic grade line, constitutes the *Piezometric height*, and measures the hydraulic pressure at that point. It will be seen that the solution of problems relating to the flow of water through pipes, lies in the knowing or ascertaining of the piezometric height at any desired point. In general, it is necessary to establish the piezometric height for every point of change of any kind which occurs throughout the entire length of the conduit. The joining of the upper extremities of these heights gives the complete hydraulic grade line.

The object of the following papers is to establish systematic methods for tracing the hydraulic grade line under the different circumstances likely to occur in practice, and generally, to furnish solutions for a large number of practical problems, commencing with the simplest cases and extending to some rather intricate ones, not usually embraced in our hydraulic manuals.

E. S. G.

Scranton, Pa., May, 1889.

TABLE OF CONTENTS.

HYDRAULIC FORMULÆ.

CHAPTER I.

Let us suppose a reservoir of large relative area and capacity to be tapped near its bottom by a horizontal cylindrical pipe, of which the length is equal to about three times its diameter.

If there were no physical resistance to the flow, the velocity of the water issuing from the pipe would be given by the formula for the velocity of falling bodies:

$$V = \sqrt{2\,g\,H} = 8.02 \ \sqrt{H}$$

in which V = velocity in feet per second, g = the acceleration due to gravity = 32.2 ft., and H = the height, expressed in feet, of the surface of the water in the reservoir above the center of the pipe.

Observation shows, however, that in the case cited the velocity of discharge is equal only to that theoretically due to a height of about two-thirds of H, that is:

$$V = \sqrt{\frac{4\,g\,H}{3}} = 6.55 \ \sqrt{H}.$$

The remaining third of the height is consumed in overcoming the resistance offered to entry by the edges of the orifice to the inflowing vein of water. The head necessary to overcome the resistance to entry is, therefore, about one-half of that necessary to produce the velocity of flow.

If the length of the pipe should be increased progressively and indefinitely, the velocity would be found to diminish inversely as the square root of the length. It would correspond, therefore, to a smaller and smaller percentage of the total head H. The resistance to entry diminishes directly as the velocity, and the head necessary to overcome it is always equal to about one-half of that necessary to produce the given velocity as calculated by the laws of falling bodies.

As the length of the pipe (always supposed to remain horizontal) increases, and the velocity of discharge diminishes, the sum of these two heads, i. e., one and a half times that necessary to produce the actual velocity, is no longer equal to the total head H, as we have seen to be the case when the length of the pipe is only about three diameters. What then becomes of the remainder of H? It is consumed in overcoming the frictional resistances engendered by contact of the moving water with the inside surface of the pipe. When the pipe is very long, and the velocity therefore relatively low, the sum of the velocity and entrance heads is small and by far the greater part of the total head is required to force the water through the pipe against the opposition offered to its flow. In such cases, which are those occurring most generally in practice when water is conveyed from a reservoir for the supply of a town, the velocity and entrance heads are commonly ignored, and the total head H is supposed to be available for overcoming the frictional resistances. As this occasions, however, an error—although generally a very small one—in the *wrong direction*, judgment is required in exercising this latitude. Later on we will revert to this point, but for the present, we will consider only frictional resistances, particularly since—and indeed because—in practice our assumed data are almost always sufficient to afford an ample margin to cover the neglected factors.

In what precedes we have considered a horizontal pipe issuing from a reservoir in which the surface of the water is maintained at a constant level. **In practice these** conditions rarely obtain.

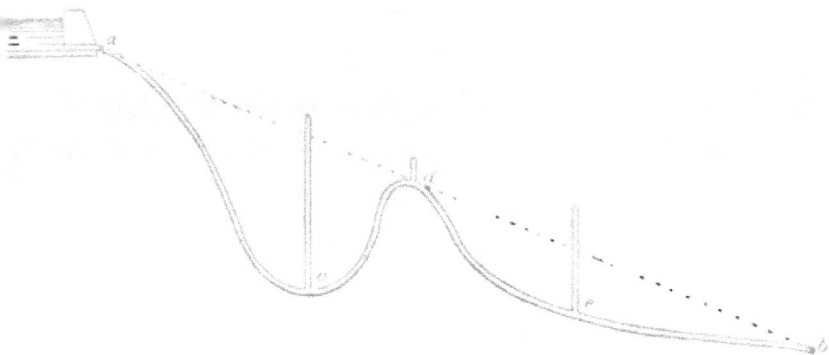

Fig. 1.

Suppose a system, **such as is shown by Fig. 1,** consisting of a **reservoir** and pipe line of varying **and contrary** slopes. As the level of **the** water in the reservoir would **be subject** to fluctuations, and liable at times to be greatly drawn down, it is customary to consider the surface of the water as standing at its lowest possible **level,** i. e., the mouth of the pipe. In this case, the **value of** H **would** be equal to the difference of level of the two extremities a and b of **the** pipe, and the line $a\,b$ joining the centers of the two ends would form what i called *the hydraulic grade line*, the **establishing** of which is the first step to be taken in laying **out a system** of water supply.

Suppose that at the points c, d, and e vertical tubes, open at their upper ends, were connected with the pipe. The water, when flowing freely from the end b of the pipe would rise in each of these tubes to about the height of the hydraulic grade line at these points, and if branches were connected at the points c, d, and e, they would, when closed, sustain a pressure upon their gates equal to the head comprised between the gates and the grade line. If the gates were open, the branches would discharge water under heads equal to the difference of level of the hydraulic grade line at the point of embranchment and their remote extremities, less a certain amount depending upon the volume discharged, which will be spoken of hereafter.

At d, where the top of the pipe just touches the grade line, there would be no pressure at all when the water was flowing through the pipe, except the very small amount due to the depth of water in the pipe itself.

If the end b should be closed so that there was no movement of water in the pipe, the water would rise in the tubes, if they were long enough, until it stood at the same level as the water in the reservoir and the pressures, at c, d, and e, would be equal to the head comprised between these points and the level of the water in the reservoir. This latter is called the *hydrostatic pressure*, or simply the *static pressure*, and the former the *hydraulic pressure*, at these points.

The tubes spoken of are known by the name of *piezometric tubes*.

The importance of correctly establishing the hydraulic grade line is illustrated by reference to a case such as is shown in **Fig. 2.** in which the pipe, at the point c, rises above the grade line $a\,b$. To explain: It will be readily deduced from what has been already said in reference to horizontal pipes that the velocity of flow, and consequently the delivery, of a pipe increases with the steepness of its slope. In this case the pipe $a\,b$ is divided into two parts-the one *a c* with a hydraulic grade line flatter than *a b* and the other *c b* with one steeper **than *a b*. The** delivery of the entire system, if the pipe were of the same diameter **throughout, would** be governed by the flatter portion ***a*** c, and the portion *c b* **would** be **capable, in** virtue **of its** steeper slope, **of discharging a greater volume of water than it could receive from** *a c.* Consequently it **would act merely as a trough and would never run full, and if a piezometric tube were placed in it at** *d,* for instance **no water would rise in the tube, and no pressure be exerted.**

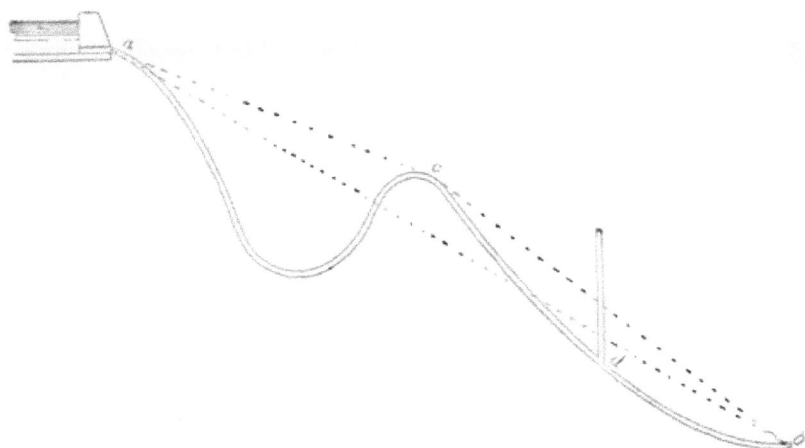

Fig. 2.

It is very important, therefore, **in locating** a pipe line **that** the pipe should nowhere rise above the hydraulic grade line. **The** full amount of water could indeed be carried over the high point *c* by means of syphonage, but this expedient is not resorted to in practice. **Should the** nature of the ground require such a location as that shown in Fig. 2, it **would be necessary to** increase the diameter of **the pipe** between *a* and *c*, so that it would deliver the re-

quired volume under the reduced head, and to diminish that between *c* and *b*, so that it should only deliver the same volume
under its increased head, and therefore run full. The calculations
necessary to determine the proper diameters will be shortly de-
veloped.

Should the axis of the pipe coincide exactly with the hydraulic
grade line *ab*, the pipe would run full (provided the feed were sufficient) but would be under no pressure, and no water would rise in
piezometric tubes placed on any part of the pipe. Moreover, as
the slope would be the same for any portion of the pipe, the
velocity and delivery would be unchanged, whether we cut the
pipe off at a comparatively short length, or extended it indefinitely.

As a further and very interesting practical illustration of the
effects of a hydraulic grade line of varying steepness, let us con-

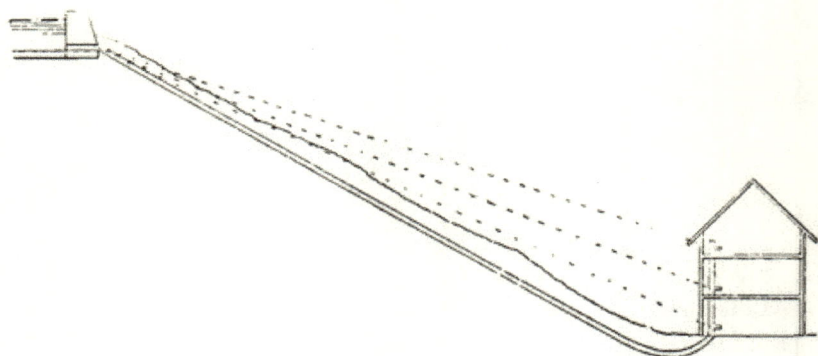

Fig. 3.

sider (Fig. 3) the case of a house supplied with water by a pipe
communicating with a reservoir.

Suppose the pipe to be just sufficiently large to furnish a certain volume of water per hour to the upper story of the house. If now a larger volume were required, it is clear that, unless we increase the diameter of the pipe, it would be necessary to increase the steepness of pitch of the grade line, in other words, to increase the head, or difference of level between the reservoir and the point of discharge. The increased volume could therefore be only drawn from a lower story.

Or, to put in same conditions under a different form, suppose, as before, the pipe to be just large enough to supply the top story of the house, the taps on the lower floors being closed. Should they be opened, it is evident that a greater amount of water would be discharged from them than from the upper one, because they would discharge under a greater head. The result would be a diminished flow, or perhaps no flow at all on the top floor, and an increased discharge of water at a lower level.

This case shows why the water ceases to rise in the upper stories of the houses of a town when the consumption increases.

It has been found by observation that the velocity of water flowing through pipes is greatly affected by the nature of their inside surface, increasing with the smoothness and diminishing with the roughness of the same. By direct experiment, coefficients have been established for different conditions of surface. It has also been found that these coefficients vary slightly with the diameter of the pipe, a pipe of a certain size giving a greater velocity than one of the same character of inside surface but of smaller diameter, the differences becoming smaller as the diameters increase.

The value of this coefficient, which will be designated throughout this paper by C, is given below for a number of different diameters and for two classes of pipes,—those which are clean and smooth on the inside, and those which are rough and incrusted, the difference being as 2 to 1. As all pipes, after a few years of service, are liable to become more or less roughened and obstructed by deposits it is always safer when calculating the proper diameters of a permanent water supply, to assume rough pipes at once, although diameters thus calculated will, for perhaps a number of years, deliver quantities greatly in excess of the desired amounts.

The coefficients given below are those determined experimentally by DARCY. Of course, in the subsequent calculations which will be made, any other values might be substituted for the ones given. It is well to remark, however, in regard to the coefficient, that although this factor is a controlling one in the calculation of the discharge of pipes, it is useless to attempt an excessive refinement in establishing its value, because not only is it difficult to determine this value with exactness for a given diameter and condition of pipe, but this condition, and even the diameter of the pipe, is liable to undergo considerable variation in the same pipe in the course of a few years.

TABLE OF COEFFICIENTS.

Diameter in inches.	Value of C for rough pipes.	Value of C for smooth pipes.
3	0 00080	0.00040
4	0 00076	0.00038
6	0.00072	0.00036
8	0.00068	0.00034
10	0.00066	0.00033
12	0.00066	0.00033
14	0.00065	0.000325
16	0.00064	0.00032
24	0.00064	0.00032
30	0 00063	0.000315
36	0.00062	0.00031
48	0.00062	0.00031

In all the following calculations, the coefficient for rough pipes will be used.

The two fundamental **equations relating to the flow of water** through long pipes are:

$$\frac{D \times H}{L} = C\, V^2 \qquad (1)$$

$$Q = A\, V \qquad (2)$$

Equation No. 2 will generally be written:

$$Q = A\, \sqrt{\frac{D \times H}{C \times L}} \qquad (3)$$

by taking the value of V from (1).

The first of these has been established by DARCY; the second is based upon a self-evident proposition.

In these equations:

D = diameter of pipe in feet
H = total head " "
L = length of pipe " "
C = coefficient
V = mean velocity in feet per second
Q = discharge in cubic feet per second
A = area of pipe in square feet = $D^2 \times 0.785$

The above **two formulae solve,** directly or indirectly, all problems relating to the **flow** through long pipes, and **all such** problems must be brought into a form admitting of **their** application, **in order to** obtain a solution.

It will be observed that $\dfrac{H}{L}$ is the **rise or fall per foot of length** of pipe, and is therefore the natural sine of the inclination of the slope to the horizon. This relation is frequently used **under the** form $I = \dfrac{H}{L}$. Using this notation, (1) would be written

$$D\, I = C\, V^2$$

In long pipes the length is generally taken as being equal to the horizontal distance separating the two ends of the pipe, as the difference between this distance and the actual length of the pipe is relatively insignificant. If, however, a case should present itself in which this difference was considerable, the actual length of pipe should be taken. Further on, an extreme case of this kind will be given, presenting some interesting features.

Some practical examples of the use of these formulæ will now be given. In all that follows, the resistances of entry, exit, and velocity will be neglected, and the total head will be considered as available for overcoming friction. The examination of cases where the above factors are included is reserved for a later portion of this paper, as they are of secondary importance when dealing with long pipes.

Example 1.—A pipe, 1 ft. in diameter and 1,000 ft. long, has a total fall of 10 ft. What are the velocity and volume of its discharge?

Substituting the given values in (1) we have :

$$\frac{1 \times 10}{1.000} = 0.00066 \ V^2$$

$$V = 3.89 \ \text{ft. per second.}$$

Using this value of V in (2), we have ;

$$Q = 0.785 \times 3.89$$

$$Q = 3.055 \ \text{cu. ft. per second.}$$

Example 2.— Two reservoirs, having a difference of level of water surface of 30 ft. are joined by a pipe 3,000 ft. long. What should be the diameter of the pipe to deliver 16 cu. ft. of water per second from the upper to the lower reservoir?

Eliminating V between (1) and (2) we have :

$$\frac{D \times H}{L \times C} = \frac{Q^2}{A^2}$$

Observing that $A = D^2\, 0.785$;

$$\frac{D \times H}{L \times C} = \frac{Q^2}{D^2 \times 0.616}$$

Whence

$$D^5 = \frac{Q^2 \times L \times C}{H \times 0.616} \qquad (4)$$

If we knew the proper value of the coefficient C in the above equation, it could be immediately solved, and the value of D obtained. But C varies with the diameter, and the diameter is as yet unknown. We must, therefore, have recourse to "Trial and Error" for a solution.

Suppose it should appear to us, at first sight, that a 12-in. pipe was likely to be of the proper size. We therefore take $C = 0.00066$, and write:

$$D^5 = \frac{256 \times 3,000 \times 0.00066}{30 \times 616}$$
$$D^5 = 27.70$$
$$D = 1.94 \text{ ft.}$$

From this we see that the pipe should be nearly 2 ft. in diameter, and as we have taken too large a coefficient (that for 24 ins. = 0.00064), we are sure that 1.94 is too large. As pipes are never made of fractional diameters, the above value of D would be taken = 24 ins., and therefore we would push the calculation no further. If the case had happened to be one requiring minute accuracy, we would recalculate the above equation, using 0.00064 for the value of C. The result would be, $D = 1.93$ ft. nearly, differing very slightly from the value already obtained.

The above examples (which are those commonly occurring in practice) are very simple, and involve only the direct application of the fundamental formulae. Let us now consider cases of a more complicated character, where they can only be used indirectly, and where a certain amount of judgment and tact is required in the preparation of the data,

Example 3.—Suppose a reservoir R (Fig. 4) containing a depth

of water of 50 ft. above the center of the horizontal pipe A, 1 ft. in
diameter and 1,000 ft. long, connected by a reducer with another
horizontal pipe B, 2 ft. in diameter and 3,000 ft. long.   It is required
to calculate the piezometric head h at the junction, from which the
discharge can be calculated, and the hydraulic grade line abc established.

Fig. 4.

It is evident that the 24-in. pipe must, under the head h, discharge the same quantity per second as the 12-in. pipe, under the
head $50-h$,   We have then from (3), the equality :

$$3.14 \sqrt{\frac{2 \times h}{3000 \cdot 0.00064}} = 0.785 \sqrt{\frac{1 \times (50-h)}{1000 \times 0.00066}}$$

Dividing by 0.785, squaring, and simplifying :

$$\frac{h}{0.02} = \frac{50-h}{0.22}$$

whence

$$h = 4.17$$

We can now very readily get the discharge, by substituting the
value 4.17 for h in either member of the above equality.   Thus :

$$Q = 3.14 \sqrt{\frac{4.17}{0.96}} = 6.51 \text{ cu. ft. per sec.}$$

Verifying in the other member—a precaution which should
never be neglected—we obtain the same result.

It is evident that the diameter of B may be assumed so large that no value of h can be found to satisfy the condition that both pipes shall run full with the given height of water in the reservoir. In such a case the pipe B serves only as a trough to receive the water discharged through A under a head of 50 ft.

Suppose that in the above example, the places of the two pipes, A and B should be changed. Evidently we should have:

$$h = 45.83$$

This piezometric height would give, with the transposed position of the pipes, the same discharge as before, the only difference being a notable change in the hydraulic grade line. If the pipes were tapped by branches, the greater elevation of the grade line in this case would bring a much greater pressure upon the branches, enabling them to deliver water at a higher level than in the first position of the pipes.

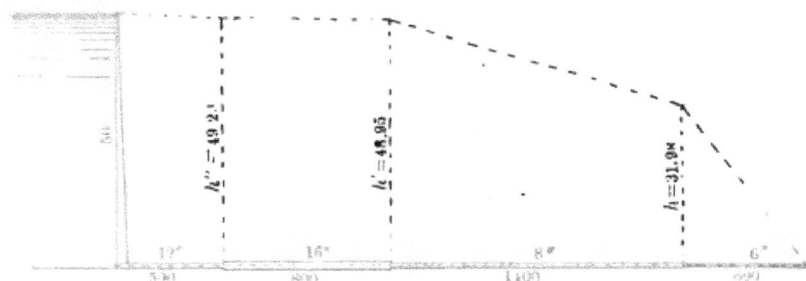

Fig 5.

The above example may be extended so as to cover cases where pipes of several different diameters are used. Thus, suppose a system of pipes, such as is shown in Fig. 5, where a reservoir with a head of 50 ft. of water, as before, is tapped by a horizontal line of pipes, consisting in order of 500 ft. of 12-in., 800 ft. of 16-in., 1,400 ft. of 8-in. and 600 ft. of 6-in., pipe.

This example may be worked in the same way as the previous one, by getting equations for h, h', and h'' expressed, by substitution, in terms of h. But it will be easier to treat the question in another way, which will also exhibit the further resources which we have at our disposal in solving hydraulic problems.

Since each section of pipe must discharge equal volumes in equal times, it is evident that the respective velocities of flow must vary inversely as the areas of the pipes.   These areas vary as the squares of the different diameters.   Designating, therefore, by V the lowest rate of velocity, i. e., that of the water passing through the largest pipe (the 16-in. one), we obtain the relative velocities in the other pipes by multiplying V by the ratio of the square of the diameter of the largest pipe, to the squares of the other diameters. It will be convenient to form the following table ;

Lengths in ft.	Diameters in ft.	Velocities in ft. per second.
500	1	1.78 V
800	1½	V
1400	⅔	4 V
600	½	7 11 V

Beginning at the lower end of the system, that is with the 6-in. pipe, and employing formula (1) in which h and V are the unknown quantities, we have.

$$\frac{1}{2} \times \frac{h}{600} = 0.00072 \times (7.11)^2 \times V^2$$

whence:

$$h = 43.68\ V^2$$

again:

$$\frac{2}{3} \times \frac{(h' - h)}{1400} = \frac{2}{3} \times \left(\frac{h' - 43.68\ V^2}{1400} \right) = 0.00069 \times (4)^2 \times V^2$$

whence:

$$h' = 67.86\ V^2$$

similarly:

$$\frac{4}{3} \times \frac{(h'' - h')}{800} = \frac{4}{3} \times \left(\frac{h'' - 66.86\ V^2}{800} \right) = 0.00065 \times V^2$$

whence:

$$h'' = 67.25\ V^2$$

Finally:

$$\frac{50 - h''}{500} = \frac{50 - 67.25\ V^2}{500} = 0.00066 \times (1.78)^2\ V^2$$

whence:

$$V^2 = 0.7321$$
$$V\quad 0.8556\ \text{ft. per second}$$

Substituting this value of V^2 in the above equations:

$$h = 31.98\ \text{ft.}$$
$$h' = 48.95\ ''$$
$$h'' = 49.23\ ''$$

We also get the velocities in the different pipes, thus:

6 inch, velocity = $7.11 \times 0.856 = 6.086$

8   "   "   = $4 \times 0.856 = 3.424$

16   "   "   = $1 \times 0.856 = 0.856$

12   "   "   = $1.78 \times 0.856 = 1.524$

The work **can be checked by using the above values of** h, h' and h'', **along with the other data, in (1), and obtaining the veloci**ties in this **way.**

Thus, beginning with the 6 inch pipe;

$$\frac{1}{2} \times \frac{31.98}{800} = 0.00072 \ V^2$$

$$V = 6.08$$

$$\frac{2}{3} \times \frac{16.97}{1400} = 0.00069 \ V'^2$$

$$V' = 3.42$$

$$\frac{4}{3} \times \frac{0.28}{800} = 0.00065 \ V''^2$$

$$V'' = 0.85$$

$$1 \times \frac{0.77}{500} = 0.00065 \ V'''^2$$

$$V''' = 1.53$$

A **very** close agreement throughout.

In the above calculations the decimals have been carried out further than **would** ordinarily **be** necessary in practice. It was **done** in the present instance **in order to** avoid discrepancies in checking.

We have another check, in **the volumes** discharged. Thus the discharge through the 6-in. pipe, **with the** given velocity is by (2).

$$Q = 0.195 \times 6.086$$
$$Q = 1.19 \text{ cubic ft. per second.}$$

All the other pipes should have an equal discharge, **for instance** the 12-in. pipe gives:

$$Q = 0.78 \times 1.523$$
$$Q = 1.19 \text{ cubic ft. per second.}$$

CHAPTER II.

In the preceding examples a series of horizontal pipes has been considered, the head being produced by an elevated reservoir placed at one end. The results would have been identical, however, if the head had been produced by the pipes being laid upon a slope, provided the difference of level between the two extremities remained the same, for the velocities and hydraulic grade line would remain unaltered. The pressure in the pipes would vary however, according to their distance below the hydraulic grade line, the pressure being measured at any given point in the pipe line, by the vertical distance between such point and the grade line. If the pipes were laid exactly upon the hydraulic grade line there would be no pressure at all in the pipes. and if they rose at any point above it, there would be either no flow or a diminished one, unless syphonage were resorted to.

In order to make this point very plain, we will consider the same system of pipes as that used in the last example, but laid as shown in Fig. 6, the upper extremity being fed by a constant supply, with only head enough to overcome resistance to entry, and produce initial velocity, which will be treated of further on.

Calculating precisely as before, we get the same hydraulic grade line, unbroken by the rising grade of the last 200 ft. of 6-in. pipe.

Fig. 6.

It is sometimes desirable to ascertain the uniform diameter of a pipe which shall be equivalent to a series of pipes of different diameters, such as we have just been studying. This may be done by an application of formula (4), which, for this purpose is written in the following form:

$$H = \frac{C\,Q^2}{0.616} \times \frac{L}{D^5}$$

As an example, let us calculate the diameter of a single pipe, of the same total length and fall as the series of pipes which we have just had under consideration, and capable of discharging an equal volume. We will first establish the general formula for all such problems, expressing the difference of piezometric level between the two ends of each pipe respectively, by $h_1\,h_2\,h_3\,h_4$, etc., their respective lengths by $l\;l_2\,l_3\,l_4$ etc., their respective diameters by $d_1\,d_2\,d_3\,d_4$ etc., and their respective coefficients by $c_1\,c_2\,c_3\,c_4$ etc. commencing with the lower end. We will express the total length by L, the total difference of level by H, the unknown diameter by D, and its coefficient by C.

Now, observing that the quantity discharged per second by each pipe is the same, we have the 4 equations.

$$h_1 = \frac{c_1\, Q^2}{0.6\,6} \times \frac{l^2}{d_1^5}$$

$$h_2 = \frac{c_2\, Q^2}{0.6\cdot6} \times \frac{l_2^5}{d_2^5}$$

$$h_3 = \frac{c_3\, Q^2}{0.616} \times \frac{l_3}{d_3^5}$$

$$h_4 = \frac{c_4\, Q^2}{0\,616} \times \frac{l_4}{d_4^5}$$

Adding, and observing that the sum of the partial heads $h_1\, h_2\, h_3\, h_4$ equals H, we have:

$$H = \frac{Q^2}{0.616}\left(\frac{c_1\, l_1}{d_1^{\,5}} + \frac{c_2\, l_2}{d_2^{\,5}} + \frac{c_3\, l_3}{d_3^{\,5}} + \frac{c_4\, l_4}{d_4^{\,5}}\right)$$

but we have also the equation

$$H = \frac{C\,Q^2}{0.616} \times \frac{L}{D^5}$$

whence, suppressing the common factor:

$$\frac{C\,L}{D^5} = \frac{c_1\, l_1}{d_1^{\,5}} + \frac{c_2\, l_2}{d_2^{\,5}} + \frac{c_3\, l_3}{d_3^{\,5}} + \frac{c_4\, l_4}{d_4^{\,5}} \tag{5}$$

The above is the general formula.

Substituting the special values of our example:

$$\frac{3300}{D^5} \times C = \frac{0.33}{1^5} + \frac{0.52}{(4\,3)^5} + \frac{0.966}{(2\,3)^5} + \frac{0.432}{(1\cdot2)^5}$$

Giving a preliminary approximate value to C of 0.00066, we have

$$\frac{2.178}{D^5} = 0.33 + 0.123 + 7.335 + 13.824$$

$$D^5 = 0.1007$$

$$D = 0.63$$

This value of D indicates a practical diameter of 8 ins.

In order to check this value, we may write (4) under the form:

$$Q = \sqrt{\frac{D^5 \times H \times 0.616}{L \times C}}$$

Substituting given values:

$$Q = \sqrt{\frac{0.1007 \times 50 \times 0.616}{2.178}}$$

$Q = 1.193$ cu. ft. per **second.**

thus proving the **correctness of the work.**

These **calculations can be abridged, and, in many cases, suffi**cient accuracy **secured by adopting** a mean common **value for** C. If we do **so in the present case,** C becomes a **common factor, and** disappears **from the calculation,** (5) becoming

$$\frac{L}{D_s} = \frac{l_1}{d_1{}^5} + \frac{l_2}{d_2{}^5} + \frac{l_3}{d_3{}^5} \text{etc.} \qquad (5)\ bis$$

If this equation be worked out for the above given values, we have :

$$D = 0.64$$

or 8 ins. as before.

It will **be observed that** this process **might have been used with** advantage **in the previous** example, **by ascertaining the dis**charge **of an equivalent** pipe, **and** then calculating **the heads** necessary to produce this discharge through the different **pipes.**

In calculating fifth powers and roots, a table of logarithms is almost indispensable. **If none is at** hand a table of squares and cubes is of some use, remembering that a number **can** be raised to the fifth power by multiplying **together its square and** cube. Fifth roots, **in** the absence of logarithms, **can** only **be** extracted by "trial **and error,"** using the above **rule for fifth powers.** [*]

Example **4th. A** horizontal pipe **(Fig. 7). 48** ins. in diameter and 2,000 ft. **long,** issues from a reservoir in **which** the surface of **the water** is maintained at a constant height of 50 ft. above the **center of the pipe.** Midway, this pipe is tapped by a branch pipe **24 ins. in diameter** and 500 ft. long, with a rising grade of 4 ft in 500.

[*] All hydraulic calculations are greatly facilitated by the use of logarithms, and those engaged in making such calculations, should not fail to familiarize themselves with the use of these powerful auxiliaries to arithmetical work.

What is the piezometric head h at the junction, and what the discharge from each pipe?*

It is evident that the 48-in. pipe above the junction must, with the head $50-h$, discharge as much water per second as the com-

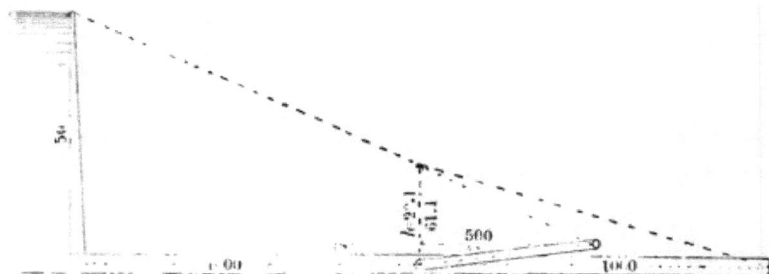

Fig. 7.

bined discharge of the 48-in. pipe below the branch with the head h, and the 24-in. pipe with the head $h-4$. From (3), which in this case will perhaps be the most convenient equation for quantity though that derived from (4) is frequently useful, we have:

$$Q = 12.56 \sqrt{\frac{4 (50 - h)}{1000 \times 0.00062}}$$

$$q = 12.56 \sqrt{\frac{4 h}{1000 \times 0.00062}}$$

$$q' = 3.14 \sqrt{\frac{2 (h - 4)}{500 \times 0.00064}}$$

which, put in equation, give:

$$12.56 \sqrt{\frac{4 (50 - h)}{1000 \times 0.00062}} =$$

$$12.56 \sqrt{\frac{4 h}{1000 \times 0.00062}} + 3.14 \sqrt{\frac{2 (h - 4)}{500 \times 0.00064}}$$

* With these given lengths and diameters, the above system does not properly come under the classification of "long pipes." As the present object is only to exemplify methods of calculation, the example is equally good.

The coefficients 0.00062 and 0.00064 are so nearly equal that **we** may, in the following calculations, discard them as common factors. Dividing by 3.14 and striking out also the common factors $\frac{2}{1000}$ and $\frac{2}{500}$, we have simply:

$$4\sqrt{50 - h} = 4\sqrt{h} + \sqrt{h - 4}$$

Squaring
$$800 - 16h = 16h + h - 4 + 8\sqrt{h^2 - 4h}$$

which gives:
$$33h = 804 - 8\sqrt{h^2 - 4h}$$

Neglecting, for a first approximate value of h **the** quantities affected by the radical:

$$33h = 804$$

Neglecting decimals:
$$h = 24.$$

Substituting this value for h under the radical:

$$33h = 804 - 8\sqrt{576 - 96}$$

which gives, always neglecting decimals, a second approximate value:

$$h = 19.$$

A third and fourth approximation give respectively $h = 20.3$ and $h = 20$.

We will take **20.1 as very near the** true value.

Substituting 20.1 in place of h in the equations giving the quantities discharged, we have:

$$Q = 12.56\sqrt{\frac{4 \times 29.9}{0.62}} = 174.45$$

$$q = 12.56\sqrt{\frac{4 \times 20.1}{0.62}} = 143.05$$

$$q' = 3.14\sqrt{\frac{2 \times 16.1}{0.32}} = 31.50$$

We have thus:
$$Q = q + q'.$$

The above method gives directly the true value of h; but it involves tedious figuring, even in our example, which happens to admit of many simplifications owing to the number of common factors. It will be easier, and often shorter, to obtain the value of h by first *assuming* one which we judge likely to be near the truth, calculating what discharge it would give from the two branches, and then calculating the head necessary to discharge the same quantity from the single pipe above the branch. Then, comparing the total height thus obtained with the known height of the water in the reservoir, we can deduce the true value of h by a proportion.

Let us apply this method to the above example. We know at once that h must be less than 25, because that would be its value if the 24-in. branch were closed. Supposing we judged that 22 ft would be about correct. We then have to solve the two equations:

$$q = 12.56 \sqrt{\frac{4 \cdot 22}{0.62}} = 149.60$$

$$q' = 3.14 \sqrt{\frac{2 \cdot 18}{0.32}} = 33.30$$

also, for the equal discharge through the 48-in. pipe above the branch, squaring (3), we have:

$$h = \frac{(182.90)^2 \times 0.62}{(12.56)^2 \times 4} = 32.87$$

This height, added to 22, the assumed value of h, gives a total height of 54.87 ft. as against 50 ft., the actual total height. By proportion we have:

$$\frac{h}{22} = \frac{50}{54.87}$$

This value of h agrees with that already found.

If the 24-in. branch were closed, we should have for the discharge:

$$Q = 12.56 \sqrt{\frac{4 \times 50}{1.24}} = 159.51$$

When the 24-in. branch was open, we had a total discharge of 174.73 cu. ft. per second. There is an increase, therefore, of **about** 9½ per cent. by opening the branch.

Let us now see **what the discharge** would be **if the branch were** placed only 500 ft. **from the reservoir, instead of 1,000 ft., all the other** conditions remaining the same.

· **We will assume** $h = 33$ ft. and solve the two equations

$$q = 12.56 \sqrt{\frac{4 \times 33}{1500 \times 0.00062}} = 149.5$$

$$q' = 3.14 \sqrt{\frac{2 \times 29}{0.32}} = 42.3$$

also

$$h' = \frac{(191.8)^2 \times 0.31}{(12.56)^2 \times 4} = 18.07$$

giving a total height **of 51.07 as against 50.** Reducing:

$$\frac{h}{33} = \frac{50}{51.07}$$

$$h = 32.3$$

Using this value, instead of the assumed **one, we have:**

$$12.56 \sqrt{\frac{4 \times 17.7}{0.31}} = 12.56 \sqrt{\frac{4 \times 32.3}{0.93}} + 3.14 \sqrt{\frac{2 \times 28.3}{0.32}}$$

$$189.83 = 148.03 + 41.76$$

very nearly.

As compared with the discharge **when** the 24-in. branch is **closed this** shows a gain of 19 per cent., **just double the** gain when the branch was located at the center of **the pipe.**

Supposing now that the branch were placed 1,500 ft. from the **reservoir.** Assuming 10 ft. as a probable value of h. we have:

$$q = 12.56 \sqrt{\frac{4 \times 10}{500 \times 0.00062}} = 142.46$$

$$q' = 3.14 \sqrt{\frac{4 \times 6}{0.32}} = 19.23$$

also:
$$h' = \frac{(161.7)^2 \times 0.93}{(12.56)^2 \times 4} = 38.53$$

By proportion
$$\frac{h}{10} = \frac{50}{48.53}$$

$$h = 10.30$$

Using this value instead of the assumed one :

$$12.56 \sqrt{\frac{4 \times 39.7}{0.93}} = 12.56 \sqrt{\frac{4 \times 10.3}{0.32}} + 3.14 \sqrt{\frac{2 \times 6.3}{0.32}}$$

$$164.13 = 144.57 + 19.68$$

very nearly.

As compared with the discharge when the 24-in. branch is closed this shows a gain of not quite 3 per cent., which is in marked contrast to the gain when the branch was only 500 ft. from the reservoir, being less than one-sixth of the gain, in that case.

It will be interesting to study a little more in detail the question of relative discharges. We have seen that when there is no branch open on the 48-in. pipe, its discharge is 159.51 cu. ft. per second. The 24-in. branches, wherever placed, increase the total discharge, but diminish that in the 48-in. pipe, below the branch. By comparing the above quantities, it will be perceived that the flow from the 48-in. pipe is diminished approximately by that proportion of the quantity flowing through the 24-in. branch which is represented by its proportionate distance from the reservoir. Thus, when the branch is 1,500 ft., or three-quarters of the length of the 48-in. pipe from the reservoir, as in the last case, its discharge is 19.62 cu. ft. per second. Three-quarters of this quantity is 14.715, which, subtracted from 159.51, leaves 144.795, or very nearly that of the 48-in-pipe below the branch, as determined by calculation.

In the same way half of the discharge, when the branch is situated half way from the reservoir, subtracted from 159.51, gives also very nearly the amount discharged below the branch. When the branch is 500 ft., or one-quarter of the total distance from the reservoir, one quarter of its discharge taken from 159.51 gives very closely the discharge as calculated for the 48-in. pipe below the branch.

Let us now take an extreme position for the branch, and suppose it placed close to the reservoir, so that there is practically no portion of the 48-in pipe between it and the reservoir. There will, therefore, be no part of the flow from the branch subtracted from that of the main pipe, and the two will each discharge the same quantity as if the other were not there. That is, the 48-in pipe will discharge 159.51, and the 24-in. 53.24 cu. ft. per second.

If we should take another extreme position for the branch, and suppose it placed at the end of the 48 in pipe, it is obvious that, with its assumed rising grade of 4-ft. in 500, it would discharge no water at all. A position could be found by trial where it would just cease to discharge water, but for the object of the present investigation this is not necessary.

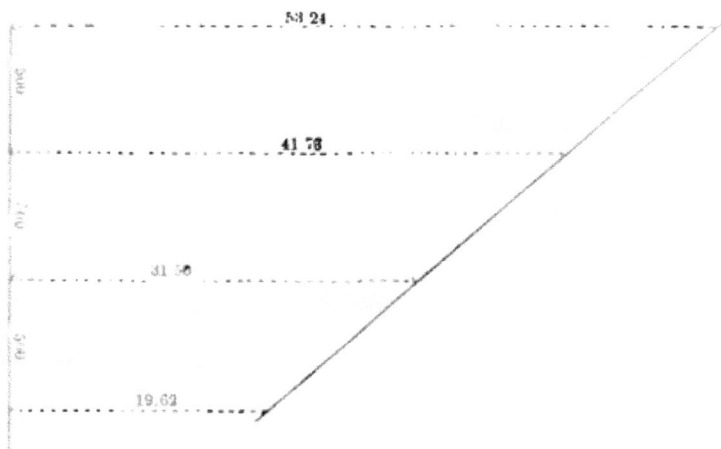

Fig. 8.

If the above results are plotted, as in Fig. 8, a very instructive diagram is obtained. The successive 500 ft. lengths being laid off as abscissæ, and the discharges measured upon the corresponding ordinates, it will be seen that their extremities all lie nearly in the same straight line.   If, therefore, the discharges for any two positions of the branch be calculated, and a straight line drawn passing through their extremities, the discharge for any other position of the branch can be obtained by erecting an ordinate at the given point to the straight line, and the flow through the main also obtained by subtracting the proper portion of that of the branch.

In practice, when making calculations similar to those under consideration, one error must be carefully guarded against namely, the supposing that the actual results will be exactly as calculated.   The chief value of these calculations lies in the fact that they furnish pretty trustworthy relative results, that is, they establish fairly well in practice the fact that if a certain pipe delivers a certain volume of water in a certain position, it will deliver a certain greater or less amount in another.   The actual amounts, in either case, cannot be surely determined, as they depend upon so many varying circumstances about which, even when aware of their existence, we have no exact date.

Let us next suppose a system in which the 48-in. pipe is tapped every 500 ft, by a 24-in. pipe, 500 ft. long, laid as before with a grade of 4 ft. in 500.

Assuming a height of 9 ft. for the piezometric column h nearest the tree end of the pipe we have:

$$12.56 \sqrt{\frac{4 \times 9}{0.31}} + 3.14 \sqrt{\frac{2 \times 5}{0.32}} = 12.56 \sqrt{\frac{4(h-9)}{0.31}}$$

Since the denominators under the radicals are so nearly equal we may cancel them, and making other simplifications, write:

$$\sqrt{9 + \frac{'}{8}} \sqrt{10} = \sqrt{h' - 9}$$

Whence: $h' = 20.52$

Again: $\sqrt{11.52 + \frac{1}{8}} \sqrt{33.04} = \sqrt{h'' - 20.52}$

$$h'' = 37.43$$

Also:

$$\frac{1}{16.91} + \frac{1}{8}\sqrt{66.83} = \sqrt{h''' - 37.43}$$

$$h''' = 63.79$$

By proportion we have:

$$\frac{h}{9} = \frac{50}{63.97}$$

$$h = 7.05$$

As the value of $h''' = 63.79$ differs considerably from the true value $= 50$, and as the above proportion is not exactly absolute, particularly in a somewhat complex system like the present, it is probable that the value just obtained for h is not a sufficiently close approximation to answer our purpose. We will therefore make a second calculation, using 7 as a second approximate value for h.

Carrying the calculation through precisely as above, we obtain the following values

$$h = 7.32$$
$$h' = 16.42$$
$$h'' = 29.60$$
$$h''' = 50.00$$

Calculating the various discharges under these piezometric heads, calling those through the different sections of 48-in. pipe commencing at the lower end, Q, Q', Q'', Q''' and those through the corresponding 24-in. branches, q, q', q'', we have:

$$Q = 122.05$$
$$q = 14.30$$
$$Q + q = 136.35$$
$$Q' = 136.10$$
$$q' = 27.63$$
$$Q'' + q' = 163.73$$
$$Q'' = 163.75$$
$$q'' = 39.72$$
$$Q'' + q'' = 203.47$$
$$Q''' = 203.75$$

These results show a very close agreement.

It is worthy of note that the total discharge in this case is not greatly increased over that obtained with a single branch situated 500 feet from the reservoir. In general it will be found, as in these two cases, that when a main is tapped at a certain point by a single branch, the total discharge is comparatively slightly increased by the introduction of a series of similar branches placed below the first junction. The position of the first branch, however, has. as the above examples show, a very great influence both on the volume of discharge and the form of the hydraulic grade line. This latter feature merits careful attention.

It will be interesting to study the effect upon the flow through such a system as we have been just considering, when the conditions are somewhat changed. For instance, in the last example let us suppose that the three branch pipes, instead of having each an equal rising grade of 4 feet in their length of 500 feet, have rising grades respectively of 4 feet, 12 feet and 24 feet in 500, commencing at the lower branch, all other conditions remaining the same.

Assuming. as before, an approximate value for h of 9 feet. we get. as before

$$h' = 20.52$$

Our next equation will be :

$$\sqrt{11.52 + \frac{1}{8}} \quad \sqrt{17.04} = \sqrt{h'' - 20.52}$$

$$h'' = 35.81$$

Again :

$$\sqrt{15.29 + \frac{1}{8}} \quad \sqrt{23.62} = \sqrt{h''' - 35.81}$$

$$h''' = 56.24$$

This value is sufficiently near the given one of 50, to warrant

our using it to obtain pretty close approximate values, by proportion, as follows:

$$h = 8.00$$
$$h' = 18.24$$
$$h'' = 31.83$$
$$h''' = 50.00$$

Whence we obtain the following discharges

$$Q = 12.56 \sqrt{\frac{32}{0.31}} = 127.6$$

$$q = 3.14 \sqrt{\frac{8}{0.32}} = 15.7$$

$$Q + q = 143.3$$

$$Q' = 12.56 \sqrt{\frac{40.96}{0.31}} = 144.4$$

$$q' = 3.14 \sqrt{\frac{12.24}{0.32}} = 19.6$$

$$Q' \times q' = 164.0$$

$$Q'' = 12.56 \sqrt{\frac{51.56}{0.31}} = 166.3$$

$$q'' = 3.14 \sqrt{\frac{15.66}{0.32}} = 22.0$$

$$Q'' + q'' = 188.3$$

$$Q''' = 12.56 \sqrt{\frac{72.68}{0.31}} = 192.3$$

This shows a pretty fair agreement between the volumes discharged, the discrepancies being due to the fact that our assumed
value of h was not sufficiently close for a fine calculation. The
figures are near enough however, to serve the purpose of showing
to how small an extent, comparatively, the results are changed by
the very considerable changes made in the inclination of the
branch pipes. Later on we shall have occasion to notice more
fully the small relative changes made in the volumes discharged
through given pipes by changes of grade; for the present we will
only call attention to the slight variations produced in the hydraulic grade line, as determined by the piezometric heads.

CHAPTER III.

Numerical example of a system of pipes for the supply of a town—Establishment of additional formulæ for facilitating such calculations—Determinations of diameters—Pumping and reservoirs—Caution regarding calculated results—Useful approximate formulæ—Table of 5th powers—Preponderating influence of diameter over grade illustrated by example.—Maximum velocities. (Note.)

As a further study of a system of pipes to deliver water, let us suppose a town divided by intersecting streets into blocks 1,000 ft. sq., as shown in Fig. 9. We will suppose that the proposed water supply requires a total volume of 3 cu. ft. per second, equal to say 800,000 U. S. galls. in 10 hours.

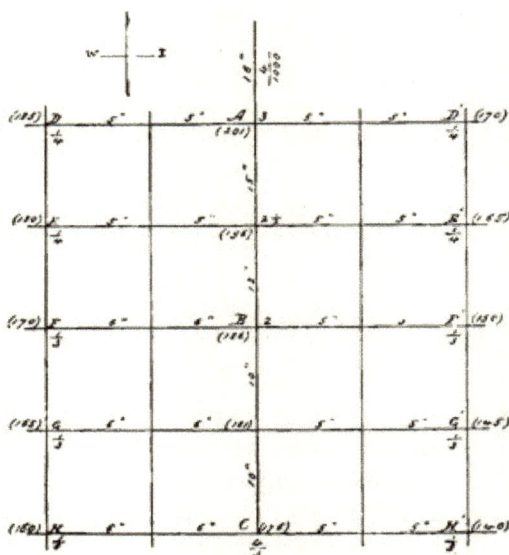

Fig. 9.

The water is to be introduced by a central main *A B C*, and delivered east and west by the side mains *D D'*, *E E'*, *F F'*, *G G'*, and *H H'*. At the extremities of these mains, the water **is to be** delivered at the elevations above datum indicated by the figures placed in brackets. **The side mains** *D D'*, and *E E'*, **are to** deliver each, **east and west,** ¼ **cu. ft. per second,** which **quantity we will** suppose is to be **carried through** the whole **length of the pipe, and** delivered **at its extremity,** without regard **to the quantities drawn off** *en route* **by the service** pipes and **smaller north and** south **mains.** This will secure a good delivery **of water** in case of **fires.** The total delivery of the above two side mains will therefore be 1 cu. ft. per second. The remaining three side mains *F F'*, *G G'*, and *H H'*, are to deliver, similarly, ⅓ cu. ft. per second at each extremity, making 2 cu. ft. for the three.

These being the **data, we will suppose the** problem **to be the** determining of the **respective diameters of the pipes, and the** height to which **the water must be raised in a supply reservoir, or standpipe, situated** somewhere **to the north of the town.**

The problem thus stated is indeterminate and **admits of an** indefinite number of solutions, for we may either use **large** pipes **and low elevations, or** small pipes and high elevations. Practi- **cally, however, there** are limitations to this; **for in** the first **place we shall naturally be restricted as** to the height to which **it would be** possible **or advisable to** raise the water, and secondly, **experience** shows **that** we should **confine** ourselves within cer- tain limits as regards the velocity **of the water** in the pipes.

Generally speaking, these velocities should **not exceed such** as would be produced by a fall of from **4 to 8 ft. per thousand, ac-** cording to the size of the pipe; the greater fall belonging to the smaller diameter. (*See note at end of chapter.*)

Before commencing the calculations, it will be **well to establish certain** additional formulæ, derived from (4), which **are frequently** of considerable utility.

When the length and diameter are constant:

$$\frac{Q'^2}{Q^2} = \frac{H'}{H}$$

When the head and diameter are constant:

$$\frac{Q'^2}{Q^2} = \frac{L}{L'}$$

When the head and length are constant:

$$\frac{Q'^2}{Q^2} = \frac{D'^5 C}{D^5 C'}$$

$$\frac{D'^5}{D^5} = \frac{Q'^2 C}{Q^2 C'}$$

When the head and discharge are constant:

$$\frac{D'^5}{D^5} = \frac{L' C}{L C'}$$

When the length and discharge are constant:

$$\frac{D'^5}{D^5} = \frac{H C}{H' C'}$$

These relations indicate that, other things being equal, the squares of the discharges vary directly as the heads and the fifth powers of the diameters, and inversely as the lengths; and that, other things being equal, the fifth powers of the diameters vary directly as the squares of the discharges and the lengths, and inversely as the heads.

As these relations are generally used for approximations, the coefficients may be dropped, and the equations written in this form :

$$Q' = \sqrt{\frac{Q^2 \times H'}{H}} \qquad (6)$$

$$Q' = \sqrt{\frac{Q^2 \cdot L}{L'}} \qquad (7)$$

$$Q' = \sqrt{\frac{Q^2 \times D'^5}{D^5}} \qquad (8)$$

$$D = \sqrt[6]{\frac{D^5 \times Q'^2}{Q^2}} \qquad (9)$$

$$D = \sqrt[5]{\frac{D^5 \times L'}{L}} \qquad (10)$$

$$D' = \sqrt[5]{\frac{D^5 \times H}{H'}} \qquad (11)$$

Other combinations can be made from these relations. Thus:

$$D = \sqrt[5]{\frac{D^5 \times H \times Q'^2}{H' \times Q^2}} \qquad (12)$$

Commencing now with the west side of the main $H H'$, we have $\frac{1}{4}$ cu. ft. to be delivered at an elevation of (160) above datum. As the pipe will be a comparatively small one, we will assume a grade of $\frac{16}{1000}$, which will give a rise of 16 ft. between the extremity and the main junction, and requires an elevation of piezometric head, at this junction, of (176), as shown in the figure

To obtain the proper diameter of pipe for this grade and discharge, we have, using (4), and assuming $C = 0.00076$ as a probable value:

$$D^5 = \frac{(\frac{1}{4})^2 \times 1000 \times 0.00076}{8 \times 0.61}$$

whence $D^5 = 0.017304$
and $D = 0.444$.

Or, for the next highest even inch:
$$D = 6 \text{ inches.}$$

As regards the diameter of the pipe on the east side, since the length and discharge are the same as for the west side, and only the heads vary, being respectively 16 and 36 ft., it can be obtained by means of (11).

Thus:
$$D = \sqrt[5]{\frac{0.6.7401 \times 16}{36}}$$
$$D = 0.3777$$

or, for next highest even inch:
$$D = 5 \text{ inches.}$$

The above head of **18** ft. per thousand produces a velocity of flow in a 5 in. pipe of a little over 3 ft. per second, which is somewhat greater than it should be. If the limit of velocity is overstepped to any considerable degree in a system of pipes such as we are considering, it would be best to use a larger pipe and check its flow down to the desired delivery by means of a gate or stop cock placed near its upper end, the effect of which will be to diminish the head. In the present instance, the excess of velocity is probably not sufficient to render this precaution necessary.

The elevations are such that the above diameters of 6 and 5 ins. are also proper for the side mains G G', F F'.

It is now necessary to calculate the diameter of the central main from B to C. This main might be divided into two parts, that between F F' and G G' and that between G G' and H H', but we will calculate it on the supposition of a uniform diameter, capable of delivering the entire volume of ¾ cu. ft. per second as far as H H'.

Assuming a probable value of $C = 0.00066$, we have from (4):

$$D^5 = \frac{16}{9} \cdot 1.32$$

whence:
$$D^5 = 0.3847$$

and:
$$D = 0.826 = 10 \text{ ins.}$$

Taking now the mains E E' and D D', and beginning on the west side, assuming as before a grade of 8 ft. per 1,000, we find the length and head equal to those of F F' etc. the only difference being the quantity it is desired to deliver, which is now ¼ cu. ft. as against ⅓ in F F'. The relation (9) is therefore applicable, and we have:

$$D = \sqrt[5]{\frac{0.017304 \times \frac{1}{16}}{\frac{1}{9}}}$$

whence:
$$D^5 = 0.0097335$$

and $D = 0.395$

or, say, $D = 5$ ins.

The mains on the east side are determined as **before**:

$$D = \sqrt[5]{0.0097345 \times \frac{16}{31}}$$

$$D = 0.346$$

This is not quite 4½ ins. but to ensure the desired delivery, it will be best to take the next highest even inch, and call it 5 ins.

As regards the central main from A to B, we find two grades, the upper one $\frac{5}{1000}$ and the lower $\frac{4}{1000}$. The lower section must deliver, under a grade of $\frac{4}{1000}$, all the water required for $F F'$, $G G'$, and $H H'$, aggregating 2 cu. ft. per second. Using (4), and taking 0.00066 as a probable value of C we have:

$$D^5 = \frac{4 \times 0.66}{6.1}$$

whence: $D^5 = 0.4328$

and: $D = 0.846$

This is very nearly 10¼ ins., and a 10 in. pipe **would answer,** though 12 ins. would be better.

The upper section must deliver 2.5 cu. ft. per second, under a grade of $\frac{5}{1000}$. **Taking the same** probable value of C, we have:

$$D^5 = \frac{6.25 \times 0.66}{2.05}$$

whence: $D = 1.237$

which we **can take as either 15 or 16 ins.**

This diameter might have been obtained from that of the lower section, by means of (12). Thus:

$$D^5 = 0.4328 \times \frac{10}{5} \times \frac{6.25}{4}$$

$$D = 1.237$$

This last formula might have been used throughout, but (4) is about as short and convenient; frequently more so.

The diameters being thus determined, the quantities should be verified by (3). They will be found somewhat in excess of those proposed, owing to the general increase of the diameters.

As regards the height to which the water must be raised, the data show that 3 cu. ft. per second must be raised to a sufficient height to reach D D' at an elevation of (201) above datum. If we adopt a grade of $\frac{1}{1000}$, the proper diameter of the pipe would be:

$$D^5 = \frac{9 \times 0.65}{2.44}$$
$$D = 1.32$$

or:

$$D = 16 \text{ ins.}$$

If, instead of pumping, the water were collected in a reservoir by damming up the natural flow of some stream, and the dam were of necessity situated at an elevation so great that a dangerous pressure is apprehended, it would be necessary to first receive the water into a distributing reservoir situated at a lower level, or else, as a less advantageous expedient, to reduce the pressure by gates, properly located for the purpose.

It should be well understood that all the above assumed data, particularly such as relate to heads, are subjected to considerable variation in actual practice. All the calculations have been based, of necessity, upon the hypothesis that the exact allotted volume per second is being simultaneously drawn from the whole system. This would rarely be the case; for at any given second, the draught would be liable to fluctuate greatly from the average. Indeed, these calculations should only be regarded as fixing, with some degree of approximation, the proper relative discharges and pressures at the different points supplied.

The remaining north and south pipes should be calculated in the same way. Thus, those below F F'' on the west side discharge 1·6 cubic ft. with a grade of $\frac{5}{5000}$. This would require a 4-in pipe. The draught from these would somewhat lower the piezometric heads at their junctions with the side mains. In a fine calculation, these reductions should be worked out, as was done in the previous example of branch pipes; in general, however, and in cases where the whole supply is supposed to be **carried through to** the extremity of **the mains, as was done in the** present instance, and where a **liberal interpretation has been given to the calculation** of **diameters, this is not indispensable. At** the same time, it should **be a guiding principle of water-works engineering, that** a **few hours spent in the** office, in **what may sometimes be** considered an over **refinement of** calculation, is by no means a waste of **time, and** frequently **enables** one to make advantageous and economical modifications in a project of distribution.

It may here be noted that (12) admits of being put into a very convenient form for rapid approximations. To do this, we have **only** to calculate **the** discharge **of a pipe 1 ft. in** diameter, with **a fall of** 1 ft. per thousand, **and** to **refer all other discharges with the fall per thousand feet to it, in order to obtain the corresponding diameter. The quantity discharged by** the above **pipe is 0.961 cu. ft. per second, and the square of the** same is 0.924. **Equation (12) may** then be written :

or very nearly :

$$D = \sqrt[5]{\frac{Q^2}{H} \times 1.08}$$

$$D = \sqrt[5]{\frac{Q^2}{H}} \tag{13}$$

we have also very nearly : $Q = \sqrt{D^5 \times H}$ (14)

These last formulæ, it will be perceived, are based on the fact **that, given** a certain probable degree of roughness, a pipe **1 ft. in diameter, with a fall of 1 ft. in a** thousand, will deliver 1 cu. ft. of **water per second. If we desire to apply** them to smooth, clean pipes, we have only to *halve the co efficient* for a 12-in. pipe, which will be equivalent to writing the above formulæ thus:

$$D = \sqrt[5]{\frac{Q^2}{2\,H}} \qquad (15)$$

$$Q = \sqrt{D^5 \times 2\,H} \qquad (16)$$

These formulae will be found of very great utility in arriving quickly at approximate results. They can be advantageously used in sketching out a network of pipes such as we have just been con sidering. To facilitate their use the following table of fifth powers has been calculated. This table indicates, by inspection, the diameters in inches corresponding to the fifth roots of the right-hand side of the equations, expressed in feet.

Diameters in inches.	Fifth Powers in feet.	Diameters in ins.	Fifth Powers in feet.
3	0.000977	22	20.72
4	0.004115	24	32.00
5	0.01256	26	47.75
6	0.03125	28	69.17
8	0.1317	30	97.66
10	0.4019	32	134.9
12	1.0000	34	182.6
14	2.1615	36	243.0
16	4.214	40	411.5
18	7.594	42	525.2
20	12.86	48	1024.0

All the diameters which have been already calculated can be obtained very nearly by the use of (13). Relations (13) and (14) might also have been used in some of the previous examples.

Formulæ (13) and (14) serve to show the comparatively small influence of *grade* as affecting the volumes discharged, which point has been already alluded to, and the preponderating influence of *diameter*. Thus, we see by the above formulæ, that for a diameter of 1 ft. and a fall of $\frac{1}{1000}$, the volume of discharge is 1 cu. ft. If we wish to double this discharge by increasing the fall, we must adopt a grade of $\frac{4}{1000}$, i. e., we must quadruple the fall. If, on the other hand, we wish to produce the same result by increasing the diameter without changing the grade, we **need** only adopt a diameter of 1.32 ft. and even a little less, on account of the decrease in the coefficient. That is to say, to double the discharge, we must increase the fall 390 per cent., or the diameter 32 per cent.

NOTE.—In completion of what has been already said in this chapter (page **37**), regarding the limit of velocities for pipes of different diameters, the following table (founded upon that given by Mr. Fanning) indicates pretty closely the maximum velocities **which it** is generally advisable to produce:

Diameter in inches,	6	12	18	24	30	36	42	48
Velocity in ft. per sec.,	2.5	3.5	4.5	5.5	6.5	7.5	8.5	9.5

CHAPTER IV.

Use of formula 14 illustrated by numerical example of compound system combined with branches—Comparison of results—Rough and smooth pipes—Pipes communicating with three reservoirs—Numerical examples under varying conditions—Loss of head from other causes than friction—Velocity, entrance and exit heads—Numerical examples and general formulæ—Downward discharge through a vertical pipe—Other minor losses of head—Abrupt changes of diameter—Partially opened valve—Branches and bends—Centrifugal force—Small importance of all losses of head except frictional in the case of long pipes—All such covered by "even inches," in the diameter.

As an illustration of the use of (14) we will calculate by its aid the discharge from a reservoir, tapped at a depth of 50 ft. by a horizontal compound system consisting successively of 2,000 ft. of 12-in. pipe, 2,000 ft. of 24-in. pipe and 2,000 ft. of 12-in. Each of these three lengths of pipe are themselves tapped midway by a 6-in. pipe, laid horizontally, the one nearest the reservoir having a length of 3,000 ft; the next, 1,000 ft., and the last, 500 ft. (See Fig. 9, *bis*) All the pipes being open, it is desired to find the piezometric heads h, h', h'', h''', h'''', at each branch and change of diameter, and the volumes discharged by each branch and section of main pipe.

Beginning at the lower end and assuming 6 ft. as an approximate value of h, we have from (14), H always representing the fall per 1,000.

$$\sqrt[1]{6} + \sqrt[5]{\tfrac{5}{4}} = \sqrt[1]{h' - 6}$$
$$h' = 15.36$$

$$\sqrt[1]{9.36} = \sqrt[1]{32\,(h'' - 15.36)}$$
$$h'' = 15.65$$

$$\sqrt[1]{9.36} + \sqrt[1]{\tfrac{15.65}{32}} = \sqrt[1]{32\,(h''' - 15.65)}$$
$$h''' = 16.09$$

$$\sqrt[1]{14.08} = \sqrt[1]{h'''' - 16.09}$$
$$h'''' = 30.17$$

$$\sqrt[1]{14.08} + \sqrt[1]{\tfrac{30.9}{32}} = \sqrt[1]{h''''' - 30.17}$$
$$h''''' = 48.82$$

Comparing this value with the given height 50, we may increase **all the** preceding values of h, h', etc., in the proportion of $\frac{50}{18.82}$. But **in** practice we would not wish to reckon on the total head, and **it** would be preferable therefore to let the values stand as they are.

We will **now calculate the quantities, calling those discharged** from the successive **sections of main pipe, beginning at the** lower end, Q Q', Q'', Q''', Q'''', **and** Q''''', **and those discharged** by the branches, **beginning also at the lower end,** q, q', q'' **respectively.** **using both (3)** and (14). The results given **by (14) naturally** check **exactly,** since they depend directly upon **the** method used in determining h, h', etc.

	By (3)	By (14)
Q	= 2.39	2.45
q	= .56	.61
$Q + q$	= 2.95	3.06
q'	= 2.96	3.06
Q'	= 2.99	3.06
q	= **.65**	.70
$Q'' + q'$	= 3.64	3.75
Q'''	= 3.64	3.75
Q''''	= 3.63	3.75
q''	= .52	.56
$Q'''' + q''$	= 4.15	4.31
Q'''''	= 4.18	4.32

The above example was very favorable to the use **of (14),** because **of** the lengths **assumed for the** different pipes, but in almost all cases it will greatly reduce **the volume of** calculation, and frequently give sufficiently close **results. Indeed,** as all these calculations **are** merely approximations, and **as we** have **taken** our coefficients pretty high, it would no doubt often be found, could the actual discharges be measured, that the apparently less exact **formula** gave the more correct results.

In all the previous examples, the coefficients for rough pipes **have been** used. **It is** well **to** remember that, as is shown by **(15)** and (16), the discharge of a clean pipe of given diameter **is about 41** per cent. greater than that of a rough pipe of the same diameter; also that the diameter of a clean pipe discharging an equal volume with a rough one, will be about 88 per cent. of the latter.   Between these limits of smoothness and roughness, there are, of course, an indefinite number of gradations.

A very interesting investigation is that of a system of pipes communicating with two reservoirs, and discharging either freely in the air, or into a third reservoir situated at a lower elevation as shown in Fig. 10.

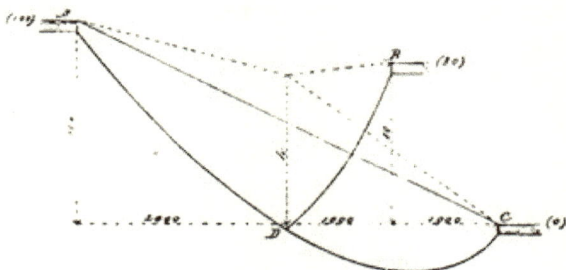

Fig. 10.

Let us suppose the water surfaces in *A* and *B* to be respectively 100 and 80 ft. above the water surface in *C*, and that all the pipes shown in the figure are 12 ins. in diameter.   Let the total length of pipe from *A* to *C* be 4,000 ft.

If communication were shut off from *B*, the flow would be direct from *A* to *C*: if communication were shut off from *C*, it would be direct from *A* to *B*.   If *A* were shut off, the flow would be from *B* to *C*.   If all the communications were wide open, we desire to know whether the flow would be from *A* to *B* and *C*, or from *A* and *B* to *C*; and in either case, to know the piezometric head *h*, at the junction *D*, and the volumes discharged.

First, let the junction *D* be situated midway in the 4,000-ft. pipe joining *A* and *C*, and let the length *B D* be 1,000 ft.   Let us for a moment revert to the supposition that *B* is shut off.   The flow would then be from *A* to *C*, the hydraulic grade line would be a straight line joining the surfaces *A* and *C*, and under our present hypothesis that the junction D is in the middle of $A\,C$, the piezometric head h would be 50 ft. above the surface of the lower reservoir C. But B is supposed to be 80 ft. above the same, and therefore the flow must be from A and B to C. We might at first sight suppose that the flow from B to C would be in virtue of the head 80 — 50 = 30 ft., which is the difference of level between B and the piezometric head at the junction; but just as a branch drawing water *from* a main pipe lowers the piezometric head at the junction, so does a branch discharging *into* the main pipe, raise it. It is necessary to see what the height h will be in the present case.

The quantity discharged into C is equal to the sum of the quantities passing from A and B. All areas and coefficients being equal, and all reductions made, we have.

$$\sqrt{\frac{h}{2}} = \sqrt{50 - \frac{h}{2}} + \sqrt{80 - h}$$

whence:

$$h = 65 + \sqrt{4.000 - 90\,h + \frac{h^2}{2}}$$

and, by successive approximations:

$$h = 74$$

Using this value of h in (3), we obtain the different discharges as follows:

$$Q = 5.88$$
$$Q' = 3.48$$
$$Q'' = 2.37$$

This gives a very close agreement in the relation $Q = Q' + Q''$.

Suppose now that the diameter of the branch $B\,D$ be reduced to 6 ins. all the other conditions remaining the same. Still regarding the co-efficients as equal, in order to get rapidly at an approximation, factoring the areas and simplifying, we have:

$$4\sqrt{\frac{h}{2}} = 4\sqrt{50 - \frac{h}{2}} + \sqrt{40 - \frac{h}{2}}$$

whence:

$$16.5\,h = 840 + 4\sqrt{8.000 - 180\,h + h^2}$$

and, by successive approximations:

$$h = 58$$

This value of h gives the following quantities:

$$Q = 5.21$$
$$Q' = 4.43$$
$$Q'' = 1.08$$

A tolerably close check, but showing that the true value of h is a little greater than the even 58 ft. at which we have placed it.

Let us now suppose that the pipe $B\ D$ is increased to a diameter of 36 ins. all the other conditions remaining as before.

Then ·

$$\sqrt{\frac{h}{2}} = \sqrt{50 - \frac{h}{2}} : 9 \sqrt{80 - h}$$

whence:
$$h = 79.90$$

Giving:
$$Q = 6.111$$
$$Q' = 3.665$$
$$Q'' = 2.816$$

a close approximation; the true value of h lies between 79.85 and 79.90.

As h increases with the diameter of the pipe $B\ D$, it might at first seem as though, by indefinitely increasing the diameter, h might be so increased as to cause a flow from A into B. A moment's reflection, however, will show that under the assumed conditions, the diameter can never be sufficiently increased to cause a flow towards B. For it has been seen that when B is shut off, the piezometric head at D is 50 ft. It is raised by opening the communication with B, and allowing water to flow into the main from B. It is evidently, therefore, an essential condition of the increase of piezometric height that the flow should be from, not to, the reservoir B.

But the effect will be different if the junction D be sufficiently advanced towards the reservoir A. Let us suppose the positions of the three reservoirs to remain the same, all the pipe diameters to be 12 ins., and the point of junction of the pipe $B\ D$ to be placed at 500 ft. from A (Fig. 11). If communication with B were shut off, the piezometric height at D would be 87.5 ft. **There would there-fore be a flow from** A to B and C when the pipe leading to B was **open.** But this flow would not take place under the head 87.5, for the draught towards B would lower it.

Fig. 11.

To ascertain the true value of h at the point D, we have **the** relation :

$$\sqrt{\frac{100-h}{500}} = \sqrt{\frac{h}{3,500}} + \sqrt{\frac{h-80}{2,500}}$$

simplifying :

$$\sqrt{100-h} = \sqrt{\frac{h}{7}} + \sqrt{\frac{h-80}{5}}$$

$$47\,h = 4060 - 11.86 \sqrt{h^2 - 80\,h}$$

whence, by successive **approximations :**

$$h = 82.65$$

Using this value of h we get :

$$Q = 5.695$$
$$Q = 4.698$$
$$Q' = .995$$

When B is shut off, in the above system, the discharge **from** A to C is 4.83 cu. ft. per second.

In all that precedes, only the resistance due to **friction has been** considered, **and the** total difference of level **between the** source of supply and **the** discharge has been taken as available for overcoming this frictional resistance. **In the** case of long

pipes, where the velocity is comparatively low, this resistance is
so greatly in excess of all the others that, in order to simplify
calculations, they are neglected. This leads to no material error
in cases where the pipe is over 1,000 diameters in length.

Attention, however, has been already called to the fact that
there are other resistances which require a certain proportion of
the total head to overcome them, leaving only the remainder
available as against friction. Indeed, it is evident if we assume
all the head to be consumed by frictional resistance alone, the water in the pipe would be in exact equilibrium, and no flow could
take place.

It will now be proper to show how the total loss of head, from
all causes, may be calculated. And first, a word in reference to
the phrase "loss of head" just employed. This term, often met
with in treatises on hydraulics, may occasionally prove confusing.
It is really little more than a convenient abbreviation. When we
speak, for instance, of "the loss of head due to velocity," we mean
the head, or fall, theoretically necessary to produce that velocity.
Similarly, when we speak of "the loss of head due to resistance to
entry," we mean the amount of head, or pressure, necessary to
force the fluid vein into the mouth of the pipe or orifice, against
the resistance of its edges. This resistance, it may be remarked in
passing, as well as that due to bends, elbows, and branches, shortly
to be mentioned, is caused by the fact that water is not a perfect
fluid, and therefore changes of direction in its flow require a certain amount of force to break or distort the form of the fluid vein
as, though to a very much less degree, would be the case with a
plastic body under similar circumstances. The property of water
which causes these resistances is called its *viscosity*.

As applied to long pipes, the principal "loss of head," and the
only one hitherto considered, is the *frictional*. The term thus applied means the height or pressure necessary to overcome the friction of the water passing with a given velocity through a pipe of

given diameter. Thus, when we speak of the frictional **loss of head** per 1,000 ft. in reference to a given pipe, we mean the fall **per 1,000 ft. necessary** to maintain the **given or desired velocity, as** against friction.

We will now investigate this subject by means of the following problem : Two reservoirs (**Fig. 12**) containing still water and **having** a difference of level of 30 ft., are joined by a pipe 12 ins. in diameter and 3000 ft. long. What is the velocity of discharge between the upper and lower reservoirs?

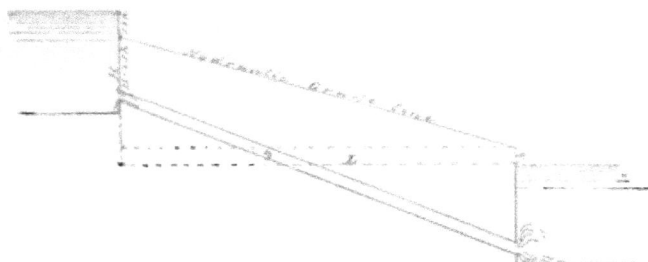

Fig. 12.

From what has been already said, it will be seen that besides the frictional loss of head, there will be the loss of head due to velocity, and that due to entrance. If the pipe discharged freely in the air at its lower end, at the vertical distance of 30 ft. below the surface of the water in the upper reservoir, these three would be the only losses of head incurred, and their sum would be equal to 30 ft.; but as the discharge takes place in a reservoir, the surface of the water in which is supposed to cover the end of the pipe, to a sufficient depth to cause the discharge to take place in still water, there is the further loss of head due to the *extinction of the velocity* which is dissipated in vortices. This loss constituted what may be called the *back pressure* of the reservoir.

In solving this problem, let us first, as heretofore, neglect **all**

losses except frictional ones.   We have then, from (1), using the
above data, and the coefficient for rough pipes:

$$\frac{1}{100} = 0.00066 \; V^2$$
$$V^2 = 15.15$$
$$V = 3.89 \; \text{ft. per second}$$

The head theoretically necessary to produce this velocity is
given by the formula derived from the law of falling bodies, $h = \dfrac{V^2}{2g}$
by substitution of the above value V.   Thus:

$$h = \frac{15.15}{64.4}$$
$$h = 0.2352$$

Besides this, there is the loss of head due to entrance.   We
have already seen that this is always equal to about half the velocity head.   We have then:

$$h + \frac{h}{2} = 0.3528$$

The loss of head from back pressure of the water in the lower
reservoir, being that necessary to extinguish the velocity must be
equal to that necessary to produce the same.   We have therefore
for the total losses, outside of friction:

$$h + \frac{h}{2} + h = 0.588$$

And the head available for overcoming friction becomes
$$30 - 0.588 = 29.412$$

We must now recast our original calculation, using 29.4 ft. instead of 30, as available frictional head.   Thus;

$$\frac{29.4}{3000} = 0.00066 \; V^2$$
$$V^2 = 14.8$$
$$V = 3.85$$

This is a very small reduction from the velocity already ob-

tained. But, in order to see how our previous solution **is affected
by the** change, we will work on new values for the **sub-heads.**
Thus :

$$h = \frac{14.8}{64.4}$$

$$h = 0.23$$

$$h + \frac{h}{2} + h = 0.575$$

$$30 - 0.575 = 29.425$$

leaving the previous value practically **unchanged.**

Let us now see, by **means of a general** formula, what is the
amount of error which we commit **when we** ignore all resistances
except friction.

Calling V the actual mean **velocity, that** is the actual volume
discharged divided by **the area of the pipe (3), we** have, in **the case**
of discharge **betweed two reservoirs, as shown in Fig. 12, the
following subheads, which together make up the total head** H:

$$H = \frac{V^2}{2g} + \frac{V^2}{4g} + \frac{V^2}{2g} + \frac{L\,C\,V^2}{D}$$

$$H = \frac{5\,V^2}{4g} + \frac{L\,C\,V^2}{D}$$

$$H = 0.039\ V^2 + \frac{L\,C\,V^2}{D}$$

That is to say, by using (3) **which gives,**

$$H = \frac{L\,C\,V^2}{D}$$

we make the error of omitting a distance **not quite equal to 4 per
cent. of the square of** the velocity.

In long pipes this is a very trifling amount.

If the pipe discharged in free air, we would have :

$$H = \frac{V^2}{2g} + \frac{V^2}{4g} + \frac{L\,C\,V^2}{D}$$

$$H = 0.0233\ V^2 + \frac{L\,C\,V^2}{D}$$

In this case we make the still smaller error of omitting $2\frac{1}{4}$ % of V^2.

In all cases, having obtained V^2 by means of (1), we can easily judge from the nature of the problem whether it is necessary to take account of these errors. In designing a system of pipes, where the problem generally is to find the proper diameter for a certain discharge, the practice of taking the next highest even inch will almost always amply suffice to cover all omissions.

As has been already stated, in all ordinary circumstances of pipe laying, the horizontal measurement of the pipe is taken instead of its actual length. It is only in special cases that this cannot be done. The extreme limit occurs in the case of a vertical pipe discharging from the bottom of a reservoir. This constitutes a very interesting special case, for should the reservoir be of indefinitely large area but of relatively shallow depth, the relation $\frac{H}{L}$ tends towards unity as L, and consequently H increases. The velocity, as determined by (1) tends therefore toward :

$$V = \sqrt{\frac{D}{C}}$$

and remains constant, no matter how greatly L may be increased. If we apply this formula to a 12-in. pipe of indefinite length, using the coefficient for rough pipes, we get,

$$V = 38.9$$

This is the maximum velocity of discharge in feet per second for a vertical 12-in. pipe under the given circumstances.

There are several minor losses of heat, besides those already considered, which are liable to occur from changes of diameter, branches, and bends or elbows. Our experimental knowledge of the effects of these features is very limited, and it is probable that much weight should not be attached to the formulæ given for their determination. A brief space will be devoted to their consideration, more with a view **to make** the present paper complete than for any practical value **which** they possess.

When water passes through a pipe of which the **diameter is abruptly changed**, at a certain point, to a greater or **a smaller one, there is a loss of head due** to the eddies **formed and** the sudden **contraction of the fluid** vein. In practice **such pipes** are always **joined by** a *reducer*, or special casting, **which forms** a tapering connection between the two. This greatly diminishes the agitation **of** the water in passing from one pipe to **the other.** It would seem however, that the mere change of velocity, independent of such agitation, causes some slight modification of the profile of the **hydraulic grade** line : and **it will be well, in any** event, **to give formulae** for the different **cases which may occur when abrupt changes take place, as these give rise to the maximum retardation. The following formulæ are taken from Claudel's** *Aide Mémoire*, **ninth edition.**

First.— When the change is from one pipe to another **of** smaller **diameter,** we have

$$h = 0.49 \frac{V^2}{2g}$$

whence :
$$h = 0.00076\ V^2$$

V **being the** velocity of the water in **the** smaller pipe. We have seen, by examples previously given, how **this** velocity may be obtained.

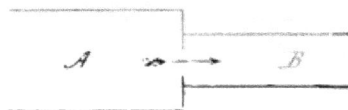

Fig. 13

Second.—If the water (Fig. 13), in its passage from the greater to the smaller pipe, passes through an opening in a thin diaphragm, as in the case of a partially opened stop-cock, we have:

$$h = \frac{V^2}{2\,g} \cdot \left(\frac{S}{0.62\,S'} - 1 \right)^2$$

in which V is the velocity in B, S the area of cross-section of B, and S', the area of the opening in the diaphragm.

Third.—When the flow is from one pipe to another of larger diameter:

$$h = \frac{(V' - V'')^2}{2\,g}$$

in which V' = velocity in small pipe, and V'' = velocity in larger one. When the water passes from a pipe into a reservoir, as in the case lately considered, V'' becomes zero, and we have, as already established in that case:

$$h = \frac{V^2}{2\,g}$$

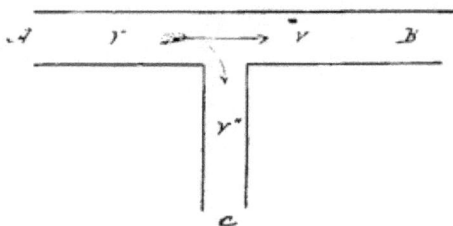

Fig. 14

Another loss of head is that due to branches (Fig. 14). In this case the water flowing from A with a velocity V', is split at the junction, part passing on towards B, with a reduced velocity V'', and part entering the branch and flowing towards C, with the velocity V'''. The loss of head occasioned by perturbations of the water at the junction has not been satisfactorily investigated. When

the branch leaves the main at a right angle, this loss, as determined by a few incomplete experiments, is :

$$h = \frac{3 \; V''^2}{2 \, g}$$

V''' being the velocity in the branch. We have already seen how
this velocity may be calculated.

If, as is generally the case in practice, the branch is deflected
gradually instead of forming an abrupt angle of 90°, the vortices
are nearly annulled, and the only loss can be from the difference
of the velocities in the three pipes. Thus for B and C respectively,
we have :

$$h = \left(\frac{V - V'}{2 \, g} \right)^2$$
$$h' = \left(\frac{V - V''}{2 \, g} \right)^2$$

For bends, or elbows, Navier's formula for loss of head is :

$$h = \frac{V^2}{2 \, g} \left(0.0128 + 0.0186 \, R \right) \frac{A}{R}$$

in which $V =$ velocity of flow, $R =$ the radius of the bend, taken
along the axis of the pipe, and $A =$ the length of the bend, also
measured along the axis.

It will readily be seen how very trifling the loss of head from
this cause will be in all ordinary cases.

The water passing around a bend exercises a radial thrust upon
it which may sometimes be so considerable as to require bracing
against. The expression for the centrifugal force F is :

$$F = \frac{M \, V^2}{R}$$

in which $M =$ the mass of the liquid in motion, $V =$ its velocity,
and $R =$ the radius of the bend measured on its axis.

As an illustration, we will suppose a pipe 24 ins. in diameter, through which the water flows with the velocity of 8 ft. per second, around a bend of 8 ft. radius.

The mass of the liquid in motion is its weight divided by g. The centrifugal force, therefore, per running foot is:

$$F = \frac{3.14 \times 62.5}{32.2} \times \frac{8^2}{8}$$
$$F = 48.72 \text{ lbs.}$$

If the bend turns a quarter circumference, its development on the axis will be 12.57 ft., and the total thrust on the bend will be $48.72 \times 12.57 = 612.4$ lbs.

This would be liable to be intensified by sudden changes in velocity, and if the bend is not well abutted, might tend to draw the joints.

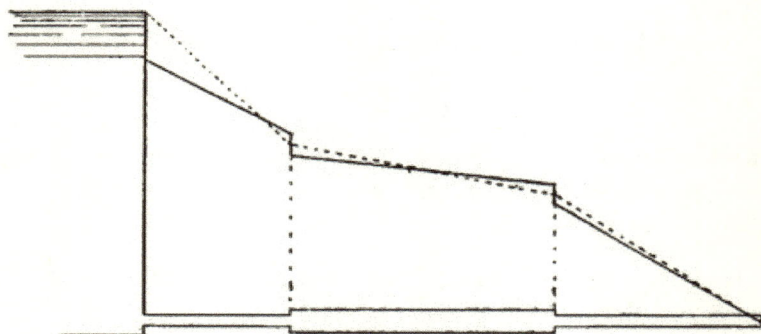

Fig. 15.

Fig. 15 shows the manner in which such losses of head as we have been just considering, modify the profile of the hydraulic grade line. The dotted line shows the grade as determined by the calculations which we have already made for a line of pipes of varying diameter. The full line, broken at the reservoir and at each change of diameter, shows the hydraulic grade as modified by losses of head due to velocity and changes of diameter. It will be understood, of course, that this is a mere random sketch, without reference to proportion.

The result of what precedes in reference to all losses of head other than friction, shows that in practice, and in the case of long pipes, such losses exercise but a trifling influence. A very small increase in the diameter of the pipe over that obtained by calculation based on frictional head alone, such as would naturally be made to get even inches, will in almost all cases largely cover all losses due to velocity, entrance, branches, bends, etc.

THE END.

www.ingramcontent.com/pod-product-compliance
Lightning Source LLC
Chambersburg PA
CBHW021529090426
42739CB00007B/852